Polar Bears

Contents

What Do Polar Bears Look Like? 2

Where Do Polar Bears Live? 6

What Do Polar Bears Eat? 8

What Do Polar Bears Do? 10

Index 16

What Do Polar Bears Look Like?

Polar bears are big bears.
They have white fur.
They have small eyes.
They have small ears.
They have sharp claws.

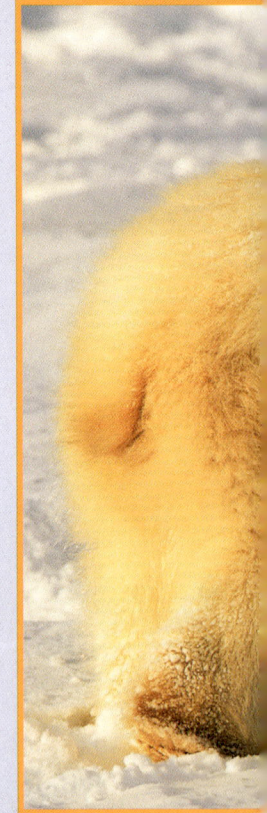

Polar bears cannot see well. They cannot hear well, but they can smell well.

Where Do Polar Bears Live?

Polar bears live on the ice and snow. They live near the sea.

KEY
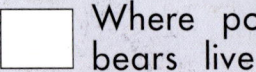 Where polar bears live

What Do Polar Bears Eat?

Polar bears eat fish. They eat seals and walruses, too.

Salmon

Seal

Walrus

What Do Polar Bears Do?

In winter, polar bears sleep in a snow den.
Cubs are born
in the den.
In spring, the cubs leave the den.

In summer, polar bears hunt seals and walruses.

They like to roll in the snow. They like to play fight. They like to sleep in the sun, too!

Index

claws	2–3
cubs	10
den	10
ears	2–3, 4
eyes	2–3, 4
food	8–9
fur	2–3
homes	6
hunt	8–9, 12–13
nose	4
sleep	10, 14